YOU CAN
NEVER BE
TOO THIN
OR
TOO RICH

YOU CAN
NEVER BE
TOO THIN
OR
TOO RICH

MARLENA SMALLBONE
AVERYL SHILKIN

ROBERT HALE · LONDON

Copyright © THIN RICH PRESS 1991
First published in Great Britain 1994

ISBN 0 7090 5425 4

ROBERT HALE LIMITED
Clerkenwell House
Clerkenwell Green
London EC1R 0HT

Text Marlena Smallbone

Illustrations Averyl Shilkin

Colour separations by Scott Repro Services
Designed and printed by Scott Four Colour Print
40 Short Street, Perth, Western Australia 6000

for Peter & David
*who make dreams
come true*

INVITATION

If you are a day-dreamer, enter
If you are full of hopes and dreams
If you wish to celebrate the joy of living
If you are weary and worn from vicissitudes
If you are a magic carpet rider, a lover of fine art
If you believe in good, beauty and inspiration
Come drink from our golden cup.

As Alice in Wonderland lives in a world where anything can happen,
So in these pages all good things happen.
Devoid of ugliness, the thoughts and images
Will uplift you, make you smile, touch your romantic spirit.

> Open at random!
> Fly when you can
> Or glance at the image only
> Set your imagination free.

What is contained within has been collected from many years of
travelling in and out of far away places, coming across rare flowers
one chances to meet in the ocean of life and records those inspiring
"bits and pieces" at timely points to help you on the way.

They will give you strength in times of joy and sorrow and inspire
you to move onward and upward.

Yours artfully,

Marlen x   *Averyl* 🌸

AVERYL SHILKIN

Averyl is West Australian born and after a nursing career enjoyed a
ten year stint as firstly a line hostess and then as hostess supervisor
with a local domestic airline.

She was recycled as an art student graduating from Claremont School
of Art. Averyl has exhibited in solo and mixed exhibitions throughout
Australia and Asia. Her main interest is etching; she is a great
defender of the decorative aspect of art and often finds inspiration
from the literature of the "nonsense" writers.

MARLENA SMALLBONE

Marlena has degrees in Anthropology and Education. She has had an action packed life travelling with the Western Australian/All Australian Netball Team, tutoring Anthropology at University, working with gifted children and travelling the world, especially the East, studying the Buddhist Way of Life. The love of beauty and inspiring words of wisdom was inherited from an early age from her mother who always read fairy tales and told her that dreams do really come true.

I am eccentric and I can do whatever I want

Prime

Just living is not enough!
One must have sunshine, freedom
and a little flower

Hans Christian Anderson

A thing of beauty

is a joy forever

John Keats

Sail forth – steer for the deep waters only,
Reckless O Soul, exploring, I with thee, and
thou with me,
For we are bound where mariner has not yet
dared to go,
And we will risk the ship, ourselves and all.

O my brave soul!
O farther, farther sail!
O daring joy, but safe! are they not all the
seas of God!
O farther, farther, farther sail!

Walt Whitman

Will you, won't you, will you, won't you,
Will you join the dance?
Will you, won't you, will you, won't you,
Won't you join the dance?

Lewis Carroll

Something we were withholding made us weak
until we found it was ourselves

Robert Frost

The Light developed
in one person
can dispel the darkness
in many others

U Ba Khin

Do not go seeking the garden of flowers!
for the garden of flowers is
in your heart – take
there your seat on the
thousand petals of the lotus,
There behold the perfect beauty

Krishna Lila Poem
Unknown Author –
15th Century

There is sweet music here that softer falls
Than petals from blown roses on the grass

Alfred Lord Tennyson

What pleases you?
I'd hock my watch
to buy you Greece
or sell my car to bring you
Rickshaws from Rangoon

Rod McKuen

Never complain and
Never explain

> *Princess Caroline of*
> *Monaco*

Judge them not harshly in a love
   Whose hold was strong
      Sorrow therein they tasted of
   And deeply, and too long

Thomas Hardy

He that clingeth to a joy
    Doth the wingeth life destroy
But he who catches it as it flies
    Lives in eternities' sunrise

Anon

The time has come the walrus said
   To speak of many things
      Of shoes and ships and sealing wax

Lewis Carroll

Are you content with what you are

right now?

Because

"right nows"

are all you have

Sujata

Warriors, warriors we call ourselves.
We fight for splendid virtue, for
        high endeavour, for sublime wisdom,
therefore we call ourselves warriors.

Aunguttara Nikaya

Then wear the gold hat,
if that will move her;
If you can bounce high,
bounce for her too,
Till she cry 'Lover, gold-hatted,
high-bouncing lover,
I must have you!'

F. Scott Fitzgerald

Our doubts are our traitors

Shakespeare

Smiles
are passports
through the desert

Rod McKuen

You can't be too thin or too rich

The Duchess of Windsor

Only the person who risks
is free

M.S.

This above all: to thine own self
be true.
And it must follow, as night the
day,
Thou canst not then be false to any
man.

Shakespeare

Hearts, like doors, will open
    with ease
To very, very little keys,
    And don't forget that two of these,
      Are "Thank you Sir", and
"If you please".

old saying

Itsy Bitsy Spider climbed up the water spout

Down came the rain and washed the spider out

Out came the sun and dried up all the rain

And Itsy Bitsy Spider climbed up the spout

again

song from childhood

"There's no use trying," she said "one can't believe impossible things."

"I daresay you haven't had much practice," said the Queen.

"When I was your age, I always did it for half-an-hour a day. Why sometimes I've believed as many as six impossible things before breakfast."

Lewis Carroll

May I be free from all suffering
    sorrow and all conflicts
May I be filled with infinite loving
    kindness, compassion, sympathetic joy
    for others and perfect equanimity
May I be fully enlightened

Buddhist Blessing

For everything you gain

you lose something

Emerson

You cannot 'fake it till you

make it'

modern cliché

*Life is what's happening to you when
you're busy making other plans*

Spinoza

Forget me not,
  I only ask
    This simple boon of thee
Oh! Let it be a simple ask
    Sometimes to think of me

old saying

"... LADY IN LAVENDER SILK"

I was seventy-seven come August,
I shall shortly be losing my bloom:
I've experienced Zephyr and raw gust
And (symbolical) flood and simoom.

When you come to this time of abatement,
To this passing from Summer to Fall,
It is manners to issue a statement
As to what you got out of it all.

So I'll say, though reflection unnerves me
And pronouncement I dodge as I can,
That I think (if memory serves me)
There was nothing more fun than a man!

Dorothy Parker

It is better to conquer yourself

   Than to win a thousand battles

Dhammapada

You may encounter many defeats
              but you must not be defeated

Maya Angelou

It's easy to smile
   when life rolls along
      like a sweet song
But the man worthwhile
   Is the man who can smile
      when everything
      goes dead wrong

Goenkaji

And now here is my secret, a very simple
    secret:
It is only with the heart that one can see
rightly; what is essential is invisible
    to the eye

Antoine de Saint – Exupéry

Some passed by with their senses
discretely averted and at the end
of their searching were impoverished

Those with "the innocent eye"
paused from time to time and
they inherited the riches of life

John Kyle

How do I love thee: let me count the ways
I love thee to the depth and breadth and height
My soul can reach . . .

Elizabeth Barrett-Browning

A bridge of love was built from soul to soul, and words could find a way along it

Herman Hesse

How many people offer
you an easy chair
in the home of their mind?

Sue Parsons

She was near and dear to him
In every feature
As the shores are close to the sea
In every breaker

Boris Pasternak

My friend to live with thee alone
   I think t'were better than to own
A crown, a sceptre or a throne

The Duke of Windsor

...one should never feel resentment against men, never judge them, because of the recollection of an act of malice, for we do not know all the good that at other times they have sincerely willed and achieved; undoubtedly the evil pattern that we have once and for all observed will come back, but the soul is much richer than that, it has other patterns also which will return

Proust

Faith – either you have it or you don't

Mother Sayama

The good writer seems to be
   writing about himself, but
      has his eye on that thread
of the universe which runs
      through himself, and all things

Ralph Waldo Emerson

*Bored people
are boring*

Lil Wightman

*There is a time for every living thing
to grow and flourish and then to die*

Ecclesiastes

You see how easily we fit together,
    as if God's own hand had cradled
    only us
and this beach town's population
    were but two . . . . .

Rod McKuen

Old love is gold love –

Old love is best

Katherine Lee Bates

Kiss me again for a lucky start,

And Happy Birthday,

with twice my heart

Ogden Nash

The moving finger writes; and
    having writ,
Moves on; nor all thy piety nor
    wit shall lure it back to cancel
    half a line,
Nor all thy tears wash out a word
    of it.

*Rubáiyát of
Omar Khayyám*

After the going out and the coming back
nothing looks quite the same

Richard Bach

Come live with me, and be my love,
And we will all the pleasures prove

Christopher Marlowe

He is Free who knows
How to keep in his own hands the
power to decide

Salvador de Madoriga

Two roads diverged in a wood, and I –
took the one less travelled by,
And that has made all the difference

Robert Frost

Sometimes gladness

Sometimes grief

Leyburn Choate

All things excellent are difficult
as they are rare

Spinoza

I yam what I yam
    that's all that I yam

Popeye, the sailor man

*How many people plant
flowers in the gardens
of their personalities?*

Sue Parsons

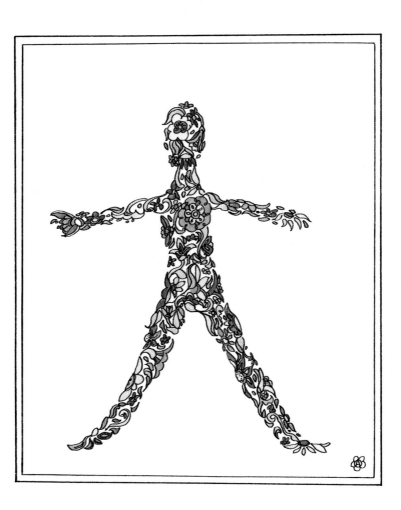

For men may come and men
    may go
        But I go on forever

                Alfred Lord Tennyson

Let me forget the tears, the silent weeping, the regrets

Françoise Sagan

Don't give up until you
Drink from the golden cup

M.S.

I came so far for beauty
　　I left so much behind

　　　　　　　Song

KID WISDOM

Are you just going out in the rain?
Yeah, we're kids

Sam Devine

Before enlightenment

           chopping wood

              carrying water

After enlightenment

           chopping wood

              carrying water

Zen Proverb

Settle one difficulty, and

You keep a hundred away

Lao-Tze

If we build our walls of self protection
high enough to be safe from hurt,
remember that love will not find a way in
either

Nanushka

Truth must triumph

U Ba Khin

There is dishonesty in any mind which demands that reality occur in a specific way

Sujata

Out of the mud the lovely lotus blossoms
Out of trials something higher vies

Raymond Ng

It takes so little effort to make such a big difference

M.S.

Star light, star bright,
    First star I see tonight,
        I wish I may, I wish I might
Have the wish I wish tonight

childhood verse

I never hated a man enough
  to give him back his diamonds

Zsa Zsa Gabor

Unless you love somebody nothing else makes any sense

E.E. Cummings

What I wanted most was love
in a straight straight forward way
I wanted you
  not as you could be
had I made you up
but the way I found you
  no different from
the way you really are

Rod McKuen

One foot cannot stand in two boots

M.S.

Life is a game of giving and receiving

M.S.

May all beings be happy and secure
May their minds be contented.
Let one not deceive another,
nor despise any person whatever
in any place.
In anger or illwill let not one
wish any harm to another

Buddhist Metta-Sutta

Happy talkie talk'in happy talk
Talk about things you like to do
You've got to have a dream
If you don't have a dream
How you gonna have a dream come true

Oscar Hammerstein II

In that Mansion used to be True-hearted
hospitality
His great fires up the chimney roared
The stranger feasted at his board

Longfellow

Now you feel no rain, for each of you
Will be shelter for the other

Now you feel no cold, for each of you
Will be warmth to the other

Now there is no more loneliness

Now you are two persons, but there is only
One life before you

Go to your dwelling, enter into the days of
your life together;

And may your days be good and long upon
the earth

Blessing
from American Indian Wedding

First thought
Best thought

Chögyam Trungpa

If you don't talk happy
And you never have a dream
Then you'll never have a
dream come true

Oscar Hammerstein II

ACKNOWLEDGEMENTS

Prime, The Duchess of Windsor, Hans Christian Anderson, John Keats, Walt Whitman, Lewis Carroll, Robert Frost, U Ba Khin, Krishna Lila, Alfred Lord Tennyson, Rod McKuen, Princess Caroline of Monaco, Thomas Hardy, Sujata, F. Scott Fitzgerald, Shakespeare, Emerson, Spinoza, Dorothy Parker, Dhammapada, Goenkaji, Herman Hesse, Elizabeth Barrett-Browning, John Kyle, Antoine de Saint-Exupéry, Maya Angelou, Boris Pasternak, Proust, Mother Sayama, Lil Wightman, Ecclesiastes, Omar Khayyam, Richard Bach, Ogden Nash, Leyburn Choate, Katherine Lee Bates, Sue Parsons, Christopher Marlowe, Salvador de Madoriga, Nanushka, Sam Devine, Lao-Tze, Zsa Zsa Gabor, Françoise Sagan, Longfellow, E.E. Cummings, Chögyam Trungpa, Raymond Ng, Aunguttara Nikaya.